SQL

Programming Basics for Absolute Beginners

Nathan Clark

Table of Contents

Any trademarks which are used are done so without consent and any use of the same does not imply consent or permission was gained from the owner. Any trademarks or brands found within are purely used for clarification purposes and no owners are in anyway affiliated with this work.

Introduction

If you're trying to dive into learning SQL, you may feel frazzled and lost. It may look like a bunch of meaningless words and texts put in random order. Rest assured, there is sense to this language and it is quite easy to navigate through when you are given the necessary tools to understand it. In a lot of ways, SQL can have many similarities to the English language itself. You just need to understand how to formulate commands in order to be successful with the language. In the same way that we formulate sentences every day in order to communicate with individuals around us, the same goes for SQL when it comes to databases.

SQL (Standard Query Language) commands structure just the way that the English language does. In this book, you will be provided with the essential knowledge in able to navigate through the program. You will learn basic commands and essential formulas in order to create tables to navigate through. You will learn what the meaning of keywords in SQL as well. You will learn the basics along with other advanced commands and what all the "nonsense" really means when put to proper use.

SQL is mostly used in order to either directly operate on the database management system or (DBMS) or to operate solely on the database management system as the use of a larger application. By the time that you thoroughly read through this book and all the information that it offers, you will begin to notice quite obvious intentions in many statements. At first, it will look like jumbled words but after a while, it will all become familiar to you. In time, it will be easier done than said in a sense.

If you are eager to learn the meaning to the jumbled mess that you are prone to seeing or you are clueless to what SQL really is, you have come to the right place. This book will go over the basics, lists of symbols and their meanings, as well as the basics to beginning with SQL. Along with the basics, this book also contains advanced statements and how to successfully use them. SQL takes time and practice just how the English language does. However, it is still possible to become familiar with the language in order to understand how it all works.

This book contains full lists of keywords, statements, commands, functions, and the formulas in order to successfully apply them. By going forward, remember to keep patience with yourself and learn to practice what you learn. Complicated things like SQL can take time and do not always have to be completely complicated.

Understanding SQL

When it comes to SQL, there is complex terminology that is hard to understand at first. In order to successfully navigate your way through the SQL language, it is important that you understand the terminology involved. By having a clear understanding of what each set of words or commands are, you can clearly formulate what each will do in the database.

- ADO- Microsoft ActiveX Data Objects

- CRUD- Acronym for CREATE, READ, UPDATE, and DELETE; the four basic commands in SQL

- Database- A collection of tables

- DBMS- Database management system

- DDL- Data definition language

- DML- Data manipulation language

- Foreign Key- A key field or column that identifies records in a table by matching a primary key in a different table

- JOIN- An SQL command used to retrieve data from 2 or more database tables with existing relationship based upon a common attribute

- ODBC- Open DataBase Connectivity- A standard database access technology developed by the Microsoft Corporation

- Primary Key- This holds a unique value which identifies each record in a table. It can be either a normal field which is a column and is guaranteed to be unique or it can be automatically generated

- Query- A request for information from a database

- RDBMS- Relational Database Management System

- SQL- Structured Query Language

- Table- A set of data which is organized in rows and columns

- Transaction- A group of SQL database commands regarded and executed as a single action

- View- A subset of columns and rows of one or more tables

With forming an SQL statement, a syntax will be used. This is best described as a "formula" when solving a mathematical equation. When forming SQL statements, it is important to remember these rules. The statements can:

- Either be in uppercase or lowercase, and are considered all identical keywords to a command. For instance, the keyword 'select' whether it is spelled in all lowercase, all uppercase, or a mixture of both, is considered all the same thing

- Continue onto the next line in order to not split words

- Be on the same line as the other statements

- Start in any column

SQL statements will consist of a number of clauses and expressions. These can be separated into two different parts. The two parts are the Data Definition Language or (DDL) and the Data Manipulation Language or (DML). The DML part in the SQL statement will be formed by the query and the update commands listed below:

- SELECT- This command will extract data from the database.

- UPDATE- This command will update data in the database.

- DELETE- This command will delete data from the database.

- INSERT INTO- This command will insert new data into the database.

When it comes to the part of DDL in an SQL statement, it will allow the tables in the database to be created or deleted. The DDL will also define indexes or keys to specify links or relationships between tables. Listed below are DDL statements in SQL that are commonly used:

- CREATE DATABASE- This will create a new database.

- ALTER DATABASE- This will modify a database.

- CREATE TABLE- This will create a new table in a database.

- ALTER TABLE- This will modify a table in a database.

- DROP TABLE- This will delete a table in a database.

- CREATE INDEX- This will create an index, also known as a search key.

- DROP INDEX- This will delete an index.

Types of SQL Comments

Comments will be used in order to clarify the purpose of SQL statements. Here are a couple of the comment types and the ways that they can be included within an SQL statement:

Line Comments

These types of comments are indicated by the presence of two hyphens (--). The text after these hyphens will be the comment. It should look like: -- with the line comment here.

Block Comments

These types of comments will be indicated by the presence of /* which will be the beginning of the comment and the end of the comment will be indicated by */. This kind of comment can cover part of the text that is in a line, or it can span multiple lines. It will look like:

/* block comment placed here */

or:

/*

block comment can

also be placed here

/

Data Types

There are certain types of data that can be found in the four main databases that SQL is used in. Listed below are the data types that can be found in each kind of database. It is important and can be very useful to have an accurate list of the very different kinds of data types.

Access Data Types

Listed below are the different types of data that can be found and used in SQL and what properties they possess and how much storage is contained.

- Byte- allows numbers from the range of 0-255 to be contained. Storage is 1 byte.

- Currency- this holds 15 whole dollar digits with additional decimal places up to 4. Storage is 8 bytes.

- Date/Time- will be used for dates and times. Storage is 8 bytes.

- Double- This is a double precision floating-point which will handle most decimals. Storage is 8 bytes.

- Integer- This will allow the amounts between -32,768 and 32,767. Storage is 2 bytes.

- Text- This is used for combinations of texts and numbers. This can up to 255 characters to be stored.

- Memo- This can be used for the text of larger amounts. It can store 65,536 characters. Memo fields can't be sorted but they can be searched.

- Long- This will allow between -2,147,483, 648 and 2,147,483,647 whole numbers. Storage is 4 bytes.

- Single- This is a single precision floating-point that will handle most decimals. Storage is 4 bytes.

- AutoNumber- This field can automatically give each record of data its own number which usually starts out at 1. Storage is 4 bytes.

- Yes/No- This is a logical field that can be displayed as yes/no, true/false, or on/off. The use of true and false should be equivalent to -1 and 0. In these fields, null values are not allowed. Storage is 1 bit.

- Ole Object- This can store BLOBS such as pictures, audio, video. BLOBs are Binary Large Objects. The storage is 1 gigabyte (GB).

- Hyperlink- This contains links to other files like web pages.

- Lookup Wizard- This will let you make an options list. A drop down list will then allow it to be chosen. Storage is 4 bytes.

MySQL Data Types

Data types can differ between different types of databases. Data is grouped into three categories:

- Character

- Number

- Date/Time

Character Data Types

- CHAR(size)- A fixed length string can be held with this data type. It is able to hold special characters, letters and numbers. This can store up to 255 characters.

- VARCHAR(size)- This can hold a variable string length which is able to hold special characters, letters and numbers. The size will be specified in parenthesis. It can store up to 255 characters. This will automatically be a text type that it is converted to if the value is placed higher than 255 characters.

- TINYTEXT- This holds a string with 255 characters of maximum length.

- TEXT- This holds a string with 65,535 characters of maximum length.

- MEDIUMTEXT- This holds a string with 16,777,215 of maximum characters.

- LONGTEXT- This holds a string with 4,294,967,295 of maximum characters.

- BLOB- These hold 65,535 bytes of maximum data.

- MEDIUMBLOB- These hold 16,777,215 bytes of maximum data.

- LONGBLOB- These hold 4,294,967,295 bytes of maximum data.

- ENUM(x,y,z, etc.)- A list that contains possible values. This list can hold 65535 max values. When a value is entered into the list that isn't contained inside that list, a blank value will be entered instead. The order that the values are entered is how they will also be sorted.

- SET- This is similar to the ENUM data type. This data type holds a maximum of 64 list items and is able to store more than one choice.

Number Data Types

The most common of the options are listed below along with their storage type when it comes to bytes and values:

- TINYINT(size)- Holds -128 to 127, or 0 to 255 unsigned.

- SMALLINT(size)- Holds -32768 to 32767, or 0 to 65535 unsigned.

- MEDIUMINT(size)- Holds -8388608 to 8388607, or 16,777,215 unsigned.

- INT(size)- Holds -2,147,483,648 to 2,147,483,647, or 4,294,967,295 unsigned.

- BIGINT(size)- Holds -9,223,372,036,854,775,808 to 9,223,372,036,854,775,807 or 18,446,744,073,709,551,615 unsigned.

- FLOAT(size,d)- This is a tiny number with a decimal point that can float. Specified in the size parameter is the maximum amount of digits. Specified in the d parameter is the maximum amount of digits in the right of the decimal point.

- DOUBLE(size,d)- This is a large number with a decimal point that floats. The maximum number of digits may be specified in the size parameter (size). The maximum number of digits to the right of the decimal point is specified in the d parameter (d).

- DECIMAL(size,d)- This type is a string that is stored which allows a decimal point that is fixed. The maximum number of digits may be specified in the size parameter (size). Specified in the d parameter is the maximum amount of digits to the right of the decimal point.

An extra option is found in integer types that is called unsigned. Normally, an integer will go from a value of negative to positive. When adding the unsigned attribute will be able to move the range up higher so that it will not start at a negative number, but a zero. That is why the unsigned option is mentioned after the specified numbers listed for the different data types.

Date/Time Data Types

The options for dates are:

- DATE()- This is in order to enter a date in the format of YYYY-MM-DD as in 2016-04-19 (April 19th, 2016)

- DATETIME()- This is in order to enter a combination of date and time in the format of YYYY-MM-DD and HH:MM:SS as in 13:30:26 (1:30 p.m. at 26 seconds)

- TIMESTAMP()- This is in order to enter to store the number of seconds and match the current time zone. The format is YYYY-MM-DD HH:MM:SS.

- TIME()- This will allow you to enter the time. The format is HH:MM:SS.

- YEAR()- This is in order to enter a year in a two or four digit format. A four digit format would be as 2016 or 1992. A two digit format would be as 72 or 13.

It is important to note that if the DATETIME and TIMESTAMP will return to the same format. When compared to each other, they will still work in different ways. The TIMESTAMP will automatically update to the current time and date of the time zone present TIMESTAMP will also accept other various formats available such as YYYYMMDDHHMMSS, YYMMDDHHMMSS, YYYYMMDD, and also YYMMDD.

Oracle Data Types

Character Data Types

- Char(size)- This stores strings of fixed lengths. The number of characters to store will be in the size parameter, with the maximum of 2000 bytes in size.

- Nchar(size)- This stores NLS strings of fixed lengths. The size is the number of characters to store with the maximum size of 2000 bytes.

- Nvarchar2(size)- This stores NLS strings of a variable-length. The number of characters to store will be in the size parameter with the maximum 4000 bytes in size.

- Varchar2(size)- This stores strings of variable lengths. The number of characters to store will be in the size parameter with the maximum size of 2 GB.

- Long- This stores strings of variable lengths. The size is the number of characters to store with the maximum size of 2 GB.

- Raw- This stores binary strings of variable lengths with the maximum size of 2000 bytes.

- Long raw- This stores binary strings of variable lengths with the maximum size of 2 GB.

Number Data Types

- Integer- This is an ANSI datatype that is equivalent to NUMBER(38).

- Int- This is an ANSI datatype equivalent to NUMBER(38).

- Smallint- This is an ANSI datatype equivalent to NUMBER(38).

- Number(p,s)- This is in order to store a number. From 1 to 38 is what it can range from -84 to 127 is what the scale can range from.

- Numeric(p,s)- This is in order to store a number. From 1 to 38 is what it can range from.

- Float- This is an ANSI datatype that is a number with a floating-point and with binary precision. The default for this data type is 126 binary or 38 decimal.

- Dec(p,s)- This is in order to store a number which can range from 1 to 38.

- Decimal(p,s)- This is in order to store a number which can range from 1 to 38.

- Real- This is an ANSI datatype to store a number with a floating-point and with binary precision. The default for this data type is 63 binary or 18 decimal. This is also equivalent to FLOAT(63).

- Double precision- This is an ANSI datatype that is a binary number with a floating point. The default for this data type is 126 binary and is also equivalent to FLOAT(126).

Large Object (LOB) Data Types

- Bfile- These are file locators that will point to the file that is binary on the system of the server file which is outside of the database. The maximum file size is of 264-1 bytes.

- Blob- This stores large objects that are binary and unstructured. These can store up to 4 GB -1.

- Clob- This stores character data of single-byte and multiple-byte. They can store up to 4 GB -1.

- Nclob- This stores unicode data. It can store up to 4 GB -1.

Date/Time Data Types

- Date- This is used to store a date anywhere between January 1st, 4712 BC and December 31st, 9999 AD.

- Timestamp- This is for storing fractional seconds' precision. It must be between 0 and 9, and 6 is the default. This includes seconds, minute, hour, day, month and year.

- Timestamp with time zone- This is for storing fractional seconds' precision. It must be between 0 and 9, and 6 is the default. This includes year, month, day, hour, minute, and seconds as well as the time zone.

- Timestamp with local time zone- This is for storing fractional seconds' precision. It must be a number between 0 and 9, and the default is 6. This includes year, month, day, hour, minute, seconds along with the expressed time zone.

- Interval year to month- This is for storing year precision and the year will be the number of digits with 2 as the default. This is for the years and months stored in the time period.

- Interval day to seconds- This is for storing day precision and must be between 0 and 9 with six as the default. This also includes the precision of fractional seconds and must also be between 0 and 9, with the default being 6. This is for a time period that will be stored in the format of days, hours, minutes, and seconds.

SQL Server

Character Data Types

- Char(n)- This is for storing a fixed-length character string. The maximum length is 8,000 characters.

- Varchar(n)- This is for storing a variable-length character string. The maximum length is 8,000 characters.

- Varchar(max)- This is for storing a variable-length character string. The maximum length is 1,073,741,824 characters.

- Text- This is for storing a variable-length character string. The maximum amount is 2 GB of data in text.

Unicode Strings

- Nchar(n)- This is for storing fixed-length unicode data. The maximum length is 4,000 characters.

- Nvarchar(n)- This is for storing variable-length unicode data. The maximum length is 4,000 characters.

- Nvarchar(max)- This is for storing variable-length unicode data. The maximum length is 536,870,912 characters.

- Ntext- This is for storing variable-length unicode data. The maximum amount is 2 GB of text data.

Binary Data Types

- Bit- This allows 0, 1, or NULL.

- Binary(n)- This is for storing fixed-length binary data. The maximum is 8,000 bytes.

- Varbinary(n)- This is for storing variable-length binary data. The maximum is 8,000 bytes.

- Varbinary(max)- This is for storing variable-length binary data. The maximum is 2 GB.

- Image- This is for storing variable length binary data. The maximum is 2 GB.

Numeric Data Types

- Tinyint- This allows 0 to 255 numbers to be stored. The storage is 1 byte.

- Smallint- This allows numbers to be stored between -32,768 and 32,767. The storage is 2 bytes.

- Int- This allows whole numbers between -2,147,483,648 and 2,147,483,647. The storage is 4 bytes.

- Bigint- This allows numbers between -9,223,372,036,854,775,808 and 9,223,372,036,854,775,807 to be stored. The storage is 8 bytes.

- Decimal(p,s)- This is for storing fixed precision and scale numbers. It allows numbers from -10^{38} +1 to 10^{38} -1 to be stored. The p parameter will indicate the digits of the maximum amount that can be stored in total. This contains both numbers to the right and left of a decimal point. A value between 1 and 38 should be assigned for the p parameter. The default is 18. The maximum amount of digits and how many can be stored to the right of the decimal point will be indicated by the s parameter. The s must be of a value of 0 to the p. 0 is the default. The storage is 5-17 bytes.

- Numeric(p,s)- This is for fixed precision and scale numbers. It allows numbers between -10^{38} +1 to 10^{38} -1. The p parameter will indicate the maximum number of digits that can be stored in total. This contains both the numbers left and right of the decimal point. The p must be a value between 1 and 38. The default is 18. The s parameter will indicate a number of digits to be stored to the right of the decimal point. The s must be a value of 0 to the p. The default is 0. The storage is 5-17 bytes.

- Smallmoney- This is for storing monetary data between -214,748.3648 to 214,748.3647. The storage is 4 bytes.

- Money- This is for storing monetary data between - 922,337,203,685,477.5808   to 922,337,203,685,477.5807. The storage is 8 bytes.

- Float(n)- This is for storing a floating precision number from -1.79E + 308 to 1.79E + 308. Whether the field should hold either 4 or 8 bytes will be indicated by the n parameter. Float (24) holds a field of 4 bytes while float(53) holds a field of 8 bytes. 53 is the default value of the n parameter. The storage will be between 4 and 8 bytes.

- Real- This is for storing a number of floating precision between -3.40E + 38 and 3.40E + 38. The storage is 4 bytes.

Date/Time Data Types

- Datetime- This is for storing a date anywhere between January 1, 1753, and December 31, 9999. This has an accuracy of 3.33 milliseconds. The storage is 8 bytes.

- Datetime2- This is in order to store a date anywhere between January 1, 0001 and December 31, 9999. 100 nanoseconds is its accuracy. The storage is 6 to 8 bytes.

- Smalldatetime- This is in order to store a date anywhere between January 1, 1900, and June 6, 2079. One minute is its accuracy. The storage is 4 bytes.

- Date- This is for storing only a date. Any date between January 1, 0001 and December 31, 9999. The storage is 3 bytes.

- Time- This is for storing only time. 100 nanoseconds is its accuracy. The storage is between 3 to 5 bytes.

- Datetimeoffset- With the addition of a time zone offset, datetime2 is the same thing. The storage is between 8 and 10 bytes.

- Timestamp- Every time that a row is either created or modified this will store a unique number. The timestamp is based on an internal clock and won't correspond with real time. Each table may only have one timestamp variable.

Other Data Types

- Sql_variant- this stores 8,000 bytes of different data types. The only data types that it will not store are text, ntext, and timestamp.

- Unique identifier- This is also known as (GUID) and will store an identifier that is globally unique.

- XML- This stores data formatted in XML. Its max is 2 GB.

- Cursor- Database operations use this to store a reference.

- Table- For later processing, this stores result set information.

The Basics of SQL and Databases

When it comes to SQL, every kind of application that manipulates data of any kind needs a place for that data to be stored. SQL serves as the database language. It is there to communicate specifically with databases. As mentioned, SQL can really be a fairly simple and easy language that can be compared to the English language. It commands structure. Databases serve as a storage mechanism. Databases allow stored information to be accessed and changed in whatever ways the storage needs to be manipulated.

Tables allow information in a database to be stored. By the use of their names and the arrangement of rows and columns, tables are able to be identified. The data type and other attributes of the column will be contained in a column. Each column will have a name. The rows will contain the data for the columns.

Tables in a database will have links or relationships between them. These relationships will either be on a one-to-one or one-to-many relationship.

The database structure is similar to spreadsheets that you find in Excel. Think of the spreadsheet as a table and each table has a name. Columns and rows work in the same way that they would in a spreadsheet. With the SQL language, it can be used to either create new tables, alter existing tables, or to fetch, update, or delete data.

When wanting to fetch any data, this action is impossible if the data is unorganized. SQL structures and organizes data. When moving text and data files and also creating relationships between tables, fetching data becomes possible with this type of organization. American National Standards Institute (ANSI) is a standard of SQL but it can be offered in other versions. In order for these versions to be (ANSI) compliant, the databases must support the main commands found in SQL: 'SELECT', 'UPDATE', 'DELETE', 'INSERT', and 'WHERE'. We will go over those commands in this beginning chapter.

The Four Basics of SQL Operations

In order to know the basics to manipulate data and tables, there are four basic operations that are necessary to understand and use to successfully use SQL. "CRUD" is what these four basic commands are often referred to in order to easily remember them.

- Create- This is in order to fill out data into tables.

- Read- This is in order to query or read data that is in a table.

- Update- This is in order to change or manipulate data that is already in a table.

- Delete- This is in order to remove data from a table.

Creating Data

In order to create or add data, you first need to be able to create a table in the database. In order to create a new table, 'CREATE TABLE' is the statement to be entered into the database. The formula as follows should be used:

CREATE TABLE table_name

(column_1 data_type,

column_2 data_type,

column_3 data_type);

You should first place the words 'CREATE TABLE'. Then, a table name should be entered. Open parenthesis should be followed by the keywords. The column name and data type should be followed by closed parenthesis where additional parameters are defined. Statements in SQL should all end with an ";" just how all English sentences end with a period.

There are a few rules that should be followed when using SQL:

- All the names of tables and columns should start with a letter.

- After the column names are properly started, numbers, letters or even underscores can follow in the rest of the column name.

- A total of 30 characters is the maximum length.

- You can't use keywords such as 'select', 'create', or 'insert' as this will confuse the database.

For instance, let's say you wanted to base your table on quotes found in books. Your table will consist of the four types of data: text, character, book, and year. This will organize the text recalled in a book, the character that in a book or that says text, the book that they can be found in and the year that the book was published. An example below is how you would create the proper table:

CREATE TABLE books_quotes

('Q_TEXT' varchar (200),

'Q_CHARACTER' varchar (20),

'Q_BOOK' varchar (20),

'Q_YEAR' number (4));

The result of this command will create an empty table that contains columns.

- 'Q_TEXT' can accept a string as long as 200 characters

- 'Q_CHARACTER' can accept a string as long as 20 characters

- 'Q_BOOK' can accept a 20 character long string

- 'Q_YEAR' can accept a listing of a year with four numbers

The next step will be to fill out the book quotes and data into the table. There are a lot of graphic interface tools for managing the tables and data used in a database. An SQL script is simply a collection of commands that are able to be executed in a sequential manner. This method can be quite useful when you have a lot of data to fill into a table. In order to insert or add a row into your database, the command is 'INSERT'. Here is the format in order to insert data:

INSERT INTO table_name

(column_1, column_2, ... column_n)

VALUES (value_1, value_2, ... value_n);

When you need to insert a row of data into a table, the keyword 'INSERT' should be followed by the keyword 'INTO' and then the table name should be entered. The parenthesis should contain the column names and be separated by commas but this is an optional step but is a good type of practice to keep in SQL. This practice will help the columns be clearly defined and that the right data is being entered into the right columns. After you have done this, you will then need to define what data will be inserted. The keyword 'VALUES' while a list of values follows and will be enclosed by parenthesis. Strings shouldn't be enclosed in single quotes. Numbers should also not be enclosed. The SQL script should look like this:

INSERT INTO Book_quotes

(Q_TEXT, Q_CHARACTER, Q_BOOK,

VALUES ('quotes placed here,

('more quotes placed here', 'and another quote',

Reading Data

You can query the data and be able to see what is stored in each table after the data is already saved into the database. You can also filter and sort the data in three different ways.

Listed below are the three statements that are highly important when querying your data into the database:

- SELECT

- FROM

- WHERE

The SELECT statement will tell the computer that you want values returned back to you and what those values are.

The FROM statement will tell you what values can be found by showing you what tables are available in the database.

The WHERE statement will list the conditions that need certain information that are to be met before it can be chosen. Until you move past the two basics, this statement can't be used.

SELECT column_1, column_2, ... column_n

FROM table_name;

In order to determine what columns will be returned to you, a declared column can be used for this function. You can use the character '*' in order to know exactly which columns are contained in a table or in order to select all the columns in a table. You can select everything in the database this way. The format would follow as:

*SELECT * FROM table_name;*

You can use the WHERE statement in order to have more specific data to match your criteria or when you don't want to select all the data contained in a table. This statement will filter the data and will retrieve data from the database that meets defined criteria. The format will be as listed below:

SELECT column_1, column_1, ... column_n

FROM table_name

WHERE column_name operator value;

As mentioned before, the WHERE statement is optional but if used, there are operators that should be used with it. Listed below is a list of operators and what they translate to in SQL:

- '='- equal to

- '>'- greater than

- '<'- less than

- '>='- greater than or equal to

- '<='- less than or equal to

- ' <>'- not equal to

- '%'- can either appear before or after specific characters or can match possible character

- 'BETWEEN'- between two values

- 'LIKE'- to search for a pattern, this can be used

- 'IN'- multiple values of possibilities in a column

The WHERE statement is able to be combined with other operators such as 'OR' and 'AND'. If you intend to use more than one of the logical operators in the same column, use the 'IN' statement instead.

An example for our book quotes using the 'AND' statement would look like:

SELECT * FROM Book_quotes

WHERE Q_BOOK = 'Book Name' AND Q_BOOK = 'Book Character';

Another example for book quotes using the 'IN' statement would look like:

SELECT * FROM Book_quotes

WHERE Q_BOOK IN ('Book Name', 'Book Character');

These essential tools have given you the ability to filter data in a database. The order in which rows were entered originally will be the same way that they are returned to you. To be able to have control over the way that the rows appear, you can sort the data by using the 'ORDER BY' statement. This statement can include one or more of the column names in a specific order. The format for this is as follows:

SELECT column_1, column_1, ...column_n

FROM table_name

WHERE column_name operator value

ORDER BY column_name;

If you want to sort book quotes by year, you can use the format below:

*SELECT * FROM Book_quotes*

WHERE Q_BOOK = 'Book Name'

ORDER BY Q_YEAR;

By default, the order in which the data in a column will be presented will be in an ascending order from lowest to highest in value. In order to change this sorting order to where it is descending, the keyword 'DESC' can be added after the column name. The format would look like the following:

*SELECT * FROM Book_quotes*

WHERE Q_BOOK = 'Book Name'

ORDER BY Q_YEAR DESC;

When it comes to the 'ORDER BY' statement it is not limited to just one column. A comma-delimited list can be included to list columns to be sorted by. The first column that is specified is the order in which the rows will be returned to you. After that column, the next columns specified will then be returned to you. The query can be written as follows:

SELECT Q_TEXT, Q_CHARACTER, Q_BOOK FROM Book_quotes

WHERE Q_BOOK = 'Book Name'

ORDER BY Q_YEAR DESC;

Update Data

You can make any changes to any data in a column and in any row after you initially enter the data. The 'UPDATE' statement can be used in order to update or change any records. The 'UPDATE' statement should be formatted as shown below:

UPDATE table_name

SET column_name = new value

WHERE column_name operator value;

When using the 'UPDATE' statement, where you place the 'WHERE' clause is very important. The 'WHERE' clause will specify which data should be updated. If the 'WHERE' clause is not executed properly when using the 'UPDATE' statement, all data in the columns will be updated and changed. A proper format should look like what follows below:

UPDATE Book_quotes

SET Q_TEXT = 'Book quote here.'

WHERE Q_BOOK = 'Book Character';

As mentioned before, if the 'WHERE' clause was left out, all of the quotes in the rows would be updated by whatever you chose.

Deleting Data

When data becomes obsolete in a database, you need to remove the data. You are able to either delete complete tables altogether or just a few rows from tables. The 'DELETE' statement should be used as follows:

DELETE FROM table_name

WHERE column_name operator value;

Just as the same rule that applies to the 'UPDATE' statement when it comes to the importance of the 'WHERE' clause, it has the same kind of importance with the 'DELETE' statement. If the 'WHERE' clause is not properly placed or is left out of the format, all of the rows and data will end up being deleted. In the instance that you want to remove a book from our database, this is how we would execute the action:

DELETE FROM Book_quotes

WHERE Q_BOOK = 'Book Name';

In the instance that you want to clean up your database and some of the tables that it contains, even all its rows, the 'DROP TABLE' statement can be used. The 'DELETE' statement is different from this statement. The 'DELETE' statement can delete all data that is contained in a table. This will leave the table by itself and its defined structure. When the statement 'DROP TABLE' is used, it will remove the table and all of the rows and data contained in it. The 'DROP TABLE' should be formatted as shown below:

DROP TABLE table_name;

To delete 'Book_quotes' from your database, you would use:

DROP TABLE Book_quotes;

Once the database is empty, it is free to be used to add new data into the system. You can use the beginning steps to add new data.

Basic Statements in SQL

With the list of data types that can be found in different kinds of databases, you can now put those data types to use. They can be used in various commands. You understand the basics of "CRUD", you can then move on to other commands.

AND/OR

In order to filter records by more than one condition, this kind of operator can be quite useful. The AND operators will display two records of the two specified conditions if the data applies to both. If a record is adequate to either the first or second condition, the OR operator will show these results.

AND

Let's say you want to look up a person by their name either first or last name, and even both. You are looking for John Smith in your database. This is how you would look up the name using the 'AND' command:

*SELECT * FROM People*

WHERE First= 'John'

AND Last= 'Smith'

OR

If you wanted to find two other individuals in a database that may have a different first name. This is where the 'OR' command comes into use.

*SELECT * FROM People*

WHERE First= 'John'

OR First= 'Robert'

This would bring up any individual in the database with the first name of "John" or "Robert" regardless of their last name.

AND & OR

These commands can be combined together in order to select individuals that have the last name that is equal to the name specified. This will select individuals with the last name considered equal to "Smith" and the first name of "John" or "Robert". This will give you a more precise search.

*SELECT * FROM People*

WHERE Last= 'Smith'

AND (First= 'John' OR First= 'Robert')

DELETE

In order to delete rows in a table, the DELETE statement can be used. It should be properly formatted as shown below:

DELETE FROM table_name

[WHERE search_condition];

Without correctly using the WHERE statement with the DELETE clause, as a result, all of the records will be deleted. To be able to remove only one individual from your table, you can use the following format:

DELETE FROM People

WHERE Last= 'Johnson'

AND First= 'Eric';

In order to delete all the rows within a table, you can use the following format:

*DELETE * FROM table_name;*

DISTINCT

When you want to eliminate any duplicate rows, you can use the DISTINCT keyword. This keyword should be formatted as shown below:

SELECT DISTINCT columns

FROM table

You can also use SELECT with the keyword DISTINCT. For instance, if you wanted to find individuals from a certain city, you can use the following format:

SELECT DISTINCT City

From People

This will bring up the distinct cities that you call for.

GROUP BY

The GROUP BY statement can be used with other functions in order to group the result of one or more columns. It should be formatted as shown below:

SELECT column_name

Aggregate_function (column_name)

FROM table_name

WHERE column_name operator value

GROUP BY column_name

The GROUP BY statement can also be used in order to find an individual's total sum. It should be formatted as shown below:

SELECT Individual, SUM (Collections)

FROM Debt

GROUP BY Individual

In order to bring up more than one column, you can use the example below:

SELECT Individual, Date, SUM (Collections)

FROM Debt

GROUP BY Individuals, Date

INSERT

In order to insert a new row into an existing table, you can use the INSERT INTO statement. The statement should be formatted as shown below:

INSERT INTO table

VALUES (value1, value2, ...)

This will only be specific to the values. It won't specify the column names of where the data will be inserted. In order to be specific of the column values along with their names, the statement should be used as shown below:

INSERT INTO table

(column 1, column 2, ...)

VALUES

(value1, value2, ...)

If you want to insert a new row into the Individuals table, it should be formatted as shown below:

INSERT INTO People

VALUES ('insert various row information here') example: (3 such as 'row 3', 'Johnson such as last name', 'David such as first name')

This allows you to insert multiple amounts of various data into different rows at the same time. In order to insert data into specified columns, such as to add and "I.D." number into rows of individuals by their first or last name, the format should be used as shown below:

INSERT INTO Individuals

(Id, Last, First)

VALUES

(5 , 'Johnson', 'Eric')

This would put information into row 5 and in the row of the last name "Johnson" and then following after, the name "Eric".

NOT

This operator can be used to negate one condition. The SELECT statement should be used with the NOT clause:

SELECT * First, Last, State

FROM Individuals

WHERE NOT (State = 'MI');

This command would bring up individuals listed in the database from every state except for Michigan.

ORDER BY

This keyword can be used to sort the order result from a specified column. By default, it will sort the data in an ascending order. In order to make it appear in descending order, use the keyword 'DESC'. The statement should be used as following:

SELECT columns

FROM table

ORDER BY sort_col [ASC | DESC];

In order to sort multiple columns, the format below should be used:

SELECT columns

FROM table

ORDER BY

Sort_col1 [ASC | DESC],

Sort_col2 [ASC | DESC],

sort_colN [ASC | DESC];

In order to sort by column positions in relevance:

SELECT columns

FROM table

ORDER BY

Sort_num1 [ASC | DESC],

Sort_num2 [ASC | DESC],

sort_numN [ASC | DESC];

In order to sort by order in descending order:

*SELECT * FROM Individuals*

ORDER BY Last name DESC

SELECT

In order to select data from a database, the SELECT statement can be used. The statement should be used in the following format:

SELECT columns

FROM tables

[JOIN joins]

WHERE search_condition]

[GROUP BY grouping_columns]

[HAVING search_condition]

[ORDER BY sort_columns];

In order to retrieve a column from a table:

SELECT column

FROM table;

In order to retrieve multiple columns from a table:

SELECT columns

FROM table;

In order to retrieve all columns from a table:

SELECT * FROM table;

In order to retrieve individuals by first and last name:

SELECT Last, First

FROM Individuals

In order to retrieve all columns from a specific table such as individuals:

SELECT * FROM Individuals

UPDATE

In order to update data that already exists in a table, the UPDATE statement can be used. It should be formatted in the following shown below:

UPDATE table

SET col1=value, col2=value2, ...

[WHERE search_condition];

All of the data in the table will be updated if the WHERE clause is used improperly in the statement. Listed below is how to properly add the WHERE clause into the UPDATE statement:

UPDATE Individuals

SET First= 'John'

City= 'Tampa'

WHERE Last= 'Smith';

WHERE

This clause should be used correctly in order to pull up specific data in a database. How to use the clause is shown:

SELECT columns

FROM table

WHERE test_col op value;

Say you want to retrieve individuals from a city:

*SELECT * FROM Individuals*

WHERE City= 'San Diego'

How to use WHERE clause with text and numeric values:

Correct:

*SELECT * FROM Individuals*

WHERE First='John'

Incorrect:

*SELECT * FROM Individuals*

WHERE First=John

Correct:

*SELECT * FROM Individuals*

WHERE Year=1965

Incorrect:

*SELECT * FROM Individuals*

WHERE Year= '1965'

CREATE DATABASE

CREATE DATABASE database_name

CREATE TABLE

The CREATE TABLE statement can be properly used as shown below:

CREATE TABLE table_name

(

column_name1 data_type,

column_name2 data_type,

column_name3 data_type,

...

)

Here is an example:

CREATE TABLE Individuals

(

Id int,

Last varchar (255)

First varchar (255)

Address varchar (255)

City varchar (255)

)

DROP

In order to delete an index that is contained in a table, the DROP statement can be used. Here is how to properly use the statement in the four main databases:

Access

DROP INDEX index_name

MS SQL Server

DROP INDEX

table_name.index_name

Oracle

DROP INDEX index_name

MySQL

ALTER TABLE table_name

DROP INDEX index_name

How to use the DROP TABLE statement:

DROP TABLE table_name

How to use the DROP DATABASE statement:

DROP DATABASE database_name

TRUNCATE

In order to remove data that is contained in a table without removing the whole table, the TRUNCATE statement can be used. The statement can be used in the format below:

TRUNCATE TABLE table_name

Advanced Statements in SQL

ALIAS

A table or column name can be given an alias when the original name is long and complex.

For tables:

SELECT column_name(s)

FROM table_name

AS alias_name

For columns:

SELECT column_name

AS alias_name

FROM table_name

You can even use an alias for individuals or a row.

How it looks without an alias:

SELECT Shipments.ID,

Clients.Last, Customers.First

FROM Clients,

Shipments

WHERE Clients.Last= 'Smith'

AND Clients.First= 'John'

How it looks with an alias:

SELECT po.Id, c.Last, c.First

FROM Clients AS c,

Shipments AS po

WHERE p.Last= 'Smith' AND

p.First= 'John'

This can make queries easier to write and read.

ALTER

In order to add, delete, or modify columns in an existing table, the ALTER TABLE statement can be used. In order to add a column to a table:

ALTER TABLE table_name

ADD column_name datatype

In order to delete a column from a table:

ALTER TABLE table_name

DROP COLUMN column_name

Keep in mind that it is important that some databases won't allow the deletion of a column by itself. In order to change the data type of a column in an existing table:

ALTER TABLE table_name

ALTER COLUMN column_name

Datatype

An example in this statement, if you want to add row of dates since your clients have been with you, you would use this format:

ALTER TABLE Clients

ADD Since date

This will add an empty new row to your Clients table and dates are able to be entered into the row. In order to change data types:

ALTER TABLE Clients

ALTER COLUMN Since year

In order to drop a column:

ALTER TABLE Clients

DROP COLUMN Since

AUTO INCREMENT/ IDENTITY

In order to allow a unique number to be created when new data is entered into a table, the AUTO INCREMENT can be used. The statement below defines the "C_Id" column to be an auto-increment key in the "Individuals" table:

CREATE TABLE Individuals

(

C_Id int NOT NULL

AUTO_INCREMENT,

Last varchar (255),

First varchar (255),

Address varchar (255),

City varchar (255),

PRIMARY KEY (C_Id)

)

This will add an auto-increment feature. The starting out number will be 1 by default when using the AUTO INCREMENT. In this way, it will increase by 1 with each new entry of data recorded. This tool can be useful for keeping track of the specific amount of entries. In order to make the AUTO INCREMENT feature start out with another value, the following format can be used below:

ALTER TABLE Clients

AUTO_INCREMENT=100

Using the AUTO_INCREMENT when inputting new data into the "Clients" table isn't necessary in order to specify a value for the column:

INSERT INTO Clients

(First,Last)

VALUES

('John', 'Smith')

Here is another statement example:

CREATE TABLE Clients

(

C_Id int PRIMARY KEY IDENTITY,

Last varchar (255) NOT NULL,

First varchar (255),

Address varchar (255),

City varchar (255)

)

The IDENTITY keyword will be used by the server in order to use the auto-increment feature. By default, the value starting out for the IDENTITY will be 1 and will increase by 1 for each new data entry. To be specific, the "C_Id" column should start out at some value or increment of some kind of specified value. You can change the identity keyword to IDENTITY by (start,increment). Using the IDENTITY is not always necessary when inputting a new data entry into the table:

INSERT INTO Clients

(First,Last)

VALUES

('John', 'Smith')

Access

CREATE TABLE Clients

(

C_Id PRIMARY KEY AUTOINCREMENT,

Last varchar (255) NOT NULL,

First varchar (255),

Address varchar (255),

City varchar (255)

)

Again, in the Access database, the default for the increment will be 1 and will increase by 1 with every new data entry. When inputting a new record of data into the "Clients" table, it isn't necessary to have a specific value for the "C_Id" column:

INSERT INTO Clients

(First,Last)

VALUES

('John', 'Smith')

Oracle

In the Oracle database system, the auto-increment field will have to be created with the sequence object. This object will generate a number sequence. In order to do this, use the CREATE SEQUENCE statement:

CREATE SEQUENCE seq_client

MINVALUE 1

START WITH 1

INCREMENT BY 1

CACHE 10

This will create a sequence that will automatically increase by 1 with each new data entry. In order to specify how many sequence values will be stored in memory and in order to attain faster access, the cache option is placed. In order to enter new data into the "Clients" table, the nextval function will be used to retrieve the next coming value from the seq_client sequence:

INSERT INTO Clients

(C_Id,First,Last)

VALUES

(seq_client.nextval, 'John', 'Smith')

This statement will insert a new record of data into the "Clients" table. In the example, the next number from the seq_client sequence will be assigned in the "C_Id" column. The "First" column would be set to "John" and the "Last" column would be set to "Smith".

BETWEEN

In order to select a range of data between two specific values, the BETWEEN operator can be used. Numbers, text, or dates can be the contained values. This operator is formatted as shown below:

SELECT column_name(s)

FROM table_name

WHERE column_name

BETWEEN value1 AND value2

Say you need to find data between the months of January and April of your "Clients" table. You would formulate the operation to look like:

*SELECT * FROM Clients*

WHERE Date since

BETWEEN 'January' AND 'April'

In different databases, the BETWEEN operator can be treated differently.

CREATE INDEX

In order to create an index that is contained in tables, the CREATE INDEX statement can be used. You can find data in a faster manner without having to read the whole table whenever you create an index. These indexes will not be visible to the user but will just be used in order to speed up searches or queries. When updating a table that contains an index, it can take more time than it would when updating a table that doesn't have an index. The cause of this is because the index needs to be updated as well any time the table data is updated. Indexes can be a useful tool for columns and tables that you know will be frequently searched.

In order to create an index:

CREATE INDEX index_name

ON table_name (column_name)

In order to create a unique index:

CREATE UNIQUE INDEX index_name

ON table_name (column_name)

This can vary between the different databases.

IN

In order to allow the specification of multiple values, the WHERE clause can be used with the IN operator. The operator should be used as shown below:

SELECT column_name(s)

FROM table_name

WHERE column_name

IN (value1, value2, ...)

In an example, if you needed to find the values recorded in two different months of your "Clients" table, you would use the statement likewise below:

SELECT * FROM Clients

WHERE Date since IN ('March', 'June')

The result would bring up the two months and the values entered in the "Date since" row.

ISNULL()

The ISNULL() function along with the NVL() and IFNULL() functions can be used in order to determine where a value is null or not. If a value is null, that means it is either invalid, void, or associated with the value of zero. Let's say you have a table chart of products listed in your inventory and you want to figure out which products that are out of stock, you could use the statement used below:

SELECT ProductName, Price * (InStock + OnOrder)

FROM Products

This will bring up quantities listed in the InStock and OnOrder rows of your chart table. In the example, if any of the values from OnOrder are null, the result will be null. In order to specify how you will want to treat any null values, Microsoft's function of ISNULL(), can be used. For other databases, the NVL() and IFNULL() can achieve the same result when used.

Access

SELECT ProductName, Price * (InStock + ISNULL(OnOrder,0))

FROM Products

Oracle

Oracle database does not have the ISNULL() function but the NVL() function can be used in order to achieve the same result that would be found in other databases.

*SELECT ProductName, Price * (InStock + NVL(OnOrder,0))*

FROM Products

MySQL

This database also does not have the ISNULL() function. To achieve the same result, the IFNULL() function can be used instead.

*SELECT ProductName, Price * (InStock +*
IFNULL(OnOrder,0))

FROM Products

LIKE

In order to search for a specific pattern that appears in a column, the LIKE operator can be used in a WHERE clause. It should be used as shown below:

SELECT column_name(s)

FROM table_name

WHERE column_name

LIKE pattern

In an example, if you have a client chart and you need to find the individuals that live in a city that starts with a specific letter, the LIKE operator can be applied as shown below:

SELECT * FROM Clients

WHERE City LIKE 'd%'

The result would bring up the cities in the client's chart that start with the letter 'd'. In order to find the cities that end with the letter 'd', you would simply reverse the percentage sign and the letter in the format. It should look like the one shown below:

SELECT * FROM Clients

WHERE City LIKE '%d'

The results would bring up all of the clients that live in cities that end with the letter 'd'. Let's say you wanted to find clients that lived in cities that had the word "land" in their name. You could use the format below in order to achieve your results:

SELECT * FROM Clients

WHERE City LIKE '%land%'

This would bring up clients that live in Portland, Orlando, and so on. By placing the percentage signs on the outside of the letters that you wish to find, you can make your search that much more specific to your needs. Let's say you wanted to do the opposite of this specific search and you wanted to find clients that lived in cities that did not contain the word "land" in the name. You could do this by using the NOT keyword in your format as shown below:

*SELECT * FROM Clients*

WHERE City NOT LIKE '%land%'

The result would bring up any clients that live in cities that do not contain the word "land" in their name.

NULL VALUES

As mentioned before, a null value will represent any missing or unknown data. As a result, a column can contain and hold null values. New data can be added or existing data can be updated without adding any value to the column if a column in a table is optional. You can do this by saving the field with a NULL VALUE. In tables, other values will be treated differently compared to null values. In order to use a placeholder for an unknown value or any value, NULL can be used. Keep in mind that NULL data and zero cannot be compared. They are not equivalent in these terms.

If you have a column that is considered an option, the data can be saved with no value in this column. As a result, it will be saved with a NULL value instead of an actual value. The only way to test and know for sure values in a chart is to use the operators IS NULL and IS NOT NULL. In order to use the IS NULL operator:

SELECT Last,First,Address

FROM Clients

WHERE Address IS NULL

The result would bring up clients in your table that have columns of null value, or columns with no data. In this case, it would bring up clients that had no address entered into the database unless there happened to be any clients with missing first or last names. In order to use the IS NOT NULL operator:

SELECT Last,First, Address

FROM Clients

WHERE Address IS NOT NULL

As a result, if what you searched before brought up clients that had no address entered into the database, this would bring up clients that did have addresses entered into the database. If there were any clients that had missing first or last name information for any reason, this would bring up any clients that had information filled out in all areas that were searched. This would bring up a list of clients with first and last names along with their address.

SELECT INTO

In order to select data from one table and insert it into another table, the SELECT INTO statement can be used. This can be useful when you need to attain backup copies of certain tables. This statement has the following formats:

In order to put all of the columns into a new table:

SELECT * INTO new_table_name

[IN externaldatabase]

FROM old_tablename

In order to select specific columns into a new table:

SELECT column_name(s)

INTO new_table_name

[IN externaldatabase]

FROM old_tablename

As mentioned, this can be useful when making backup copies of tables. Here are a few examples listed below:

In order to make an exact copy of data in the "Clients" table:

*SELECT * INTO Clients_Backup*

FROM Clients

In order to copy the table into another database, the IN clause can also be used:

*SELECT * INTO Client_Backup*

IN 'Backup.mdb'

FROM Clients

You can use the statement to only back up just a few fields to be copied into a new table:

SELECT Last,First

INTO Clients_Backup

FROM Clients

SELECT INTO with WHERE clause:

SELECT Last,First

INTO Clients_Backup

FROM Clients

WHERE City= 'Portland'

This would back up all clients that reside in the city of Portland.

SELECT INTO with joined tables:

SELECT Clients.Last,Orders.OrderNo

INTO Client_Order_Backup

FROM Clients

INNER JOIN Orders

ON Clients.C_Id=Orders.C_Id

The "Client_Order_Backup' table will result in containing data from the two tables of "Clients" and "Orders".

TOP

In order to specify the number of data that you want to be returned to you, the TOP clause can be used in order to achieve this. When working with many tables that need to be managed in a database, this can be a useful tool. Not all database systems will support the TOP clause though. It should be formatted as shown below:

SELECT TOP number | percent column_name(s)

FROM table_name

There are two ways to use this clause in MySQL and Oracle:

MySQL

SELECT column_name(s)

FROM table_name

LIMIT number

Oracle

SELECT column_name(s)

FROM table_name

WHERE ROWNUM = number

TOP NUMBER

For some examples, when you want to pull up only a certain number of clients in your table instead of the whole table, this can be done in the example shown below:

SELECT TOP 10 *

FROM Clients

The result would only bring up the top ten clients in a table instead of the whole table.

TOP PERCENT

Let's say instead of focusing on a specific number, you wanted to focus on a percentage. In this case, you want to pull up the top 25% of clients in a table:

SELECT TOP 25 PERCENT *

FROM Clients

UNION

In order to combine two or more SELECT statements, the UNION clause can be used. The same number of columns must be the same as the ones specified in the SELECT statement when using the UNION clause. The same data types must also be involved as well. In each SELECT statement, the columns also need to be the same order. They should be formed as shown below:

SELECT column_name(s)

FROM table_name1

UNION

SELECT column_name(s)

FROM table_name2

By default, the UNION operator will only select distinct values. You can use the UNION ALL statement in order to allow duplicate values:

SELECT column_name(s)

FROM table_name1

UNION ALL

SELECT column_name(s)

FROM table_name2

In the first SELECT statement when using the UNION clause, the names of the columns will always be equal. Let's say you want to bring up clients from two different cities. Let's say you want to pull up all the clients from Portland and Las Vegas:

SELECT Name

FROM Clients_Portland

UNION

SELECT Name

FROM Clients_LasVegas

The result will bring up clients in the database that live in those two specific cities. Although it seems like this would be the solution for bringing up all the clients listed in those two cities, it is not the case. This will only bring up the clients whose names are equal to each other. The UNION command will only select distinct values. In order to select all clients in two specific cities, use the UNION ALL formula shown below:

SELECT Name

FROM Clients_Portland

UNION ALL

SELECT Name

FROM Clients_LasVegas

This way, the only thing that changes compared to the previous formula is that the word "ALL" is added behind UNION and as a result, this brings up all the clients in those two specific cities.

VIEW

When using the VIEW command in SQL, it is based on the result-based table that will be shown on a virtual table. Just how a real table would appear, a view will contain rows and columns. The fields that are from one or more actual tables in the database are the fields that will appear in the VIEW function. Functions in SQL just like WHERE and JOIN can be used with the VIEW command in order to properly present the data.

CREATE VIEW

CREATE VIEW view_name AS

SELECT column_name(s)

FROM table_name

WHERE condition

Keep in mind that a view will always show data in an up-to-date form. The database engine will recreate the data in order for it to appear in a view. In order to update a VIEW:

CREATE OR REPLACE VIEW view_name AS

SELECT column_name(s)

FROM table_name

WHERE condition

In this example, the "Category" column will be added to the "Current Product List":

CREATE VIEW [Current Product List] AS

SELECT ProductID,ProductName,Category

FROM Products

WHERE Discontinued=No

The DROP VIEW command can be used in order to delete a view:

DROP VIEW view_name

WILDCARDS

In order to substitute one or more characters when searching data, wildcards can be useful for this purpose. A list of wildcards that can be used is listed below:

- %- Can be used in order to substitute for zero or more characters.

- _- Can be used in order to substitute for exactly one character.

- [charlist]- Can be used in order to match a single character from a set of characters.

- [^charlist] or [!charlist]- Can be used in order to match a single character that is not from a set of characters.

How to use the '%' Wildcard

*SELECT * FROM Clients*

WHERE City LIKE 'po%'

This would bring up cities that began with the letters, Po like, Portland. This can also be used to look for a pattern. Just how it was mentioned in the "LIKE" command section, this wildcard can be used to pull up patterns in words. If you wanted to pull up the cities that had the word "land" in their name, you could do this with the example below:

*SELECT * FROM Clients*

WHERE City LIKE '%land%'

How to use the _ Wildcard

This can be used in a way to pull up names of clients with specified letters in their name. Say you wanted to look up clients whose last name contained the letters "am". You could do this with the example below:

*SELECT * FROM Clients*

WHERE First LIKE '_am'

This would pull up names like "Campbell", "Cramer", or "Sampson". Let's say you wanted to use this wildcard to replace certain letters in different places of a last name, you could do this with the example down below:

*SELECT * FROM Clients*

WHERE Last LIKE 'J_n_s'

This would pull up data like the last name "Jones".

How to use the [charlist] Wildcard

*SELECT * FROM Clients*

WHERE Last LIKE '[cl]'

You could use this in order to pull up clients with last names that start with the letters c and l. You would pull up last names like Campbell and Lawson. If you wanted to select clients with last names that did not start with c and l, you would use the formula shown below

SELECT * FROM Clients

WHERE Last LIKE '[!cl]%'

You would not pull up last names like Campbell or Lawson. You would pull up last names like Anderson, Jones, or any last name that started with letters other than c or l.

Using Constraints in SQL

Constraints can be used in order to limit what kind of data can be entered into a table. When a table is created, specified constraints can be used. This can be done by using CREATE TABLE or ALTER TABLE statements. Below is a list of some of the more common constraints:

- CHECK- This specifies a constraint that will limit the value range that can be placed in a column.

- DEFAULT- This specifies a constraint that is used in order to insert a default value into a column.

- FOREIGN KEY- This specifies a constraint that prevents invalid data from being inserted into the foreign key column because it has to be one of the values contained in the table that it points to.

- NOT NULL- This specifies a constraint that enforces a column to not accept values that are null.

- PRIMARY KEY- This specifies a constraint that uniquely identifies each record in a database table. It is important to note that each table should have a primary key and each table can only have one primary key.

- UNIQUE- This specifies a constraint that uniquely identifies each record in a database table. It is important to note that a table can have many UNIQUE constraints, but only one PRIMARY KEY constraint.

CHECK

How to use the CHECK constraint on CREATE TABLE:

My SQL

CREATE TABLE Clients

(

C_Id int NOT NULL,

Last varchar (255) NOT NULL,

First varchar (255),

Address varchar (255),

City varchar (255),

CHECK (C_Id 0)

)

SQL Server/Oracle/Access

CREATE TABLE Clients

(

C_Id int NOT NULL

CHECK (C_Id 0),

Last varchar (255) NOT NULL,

First varchar (255),

Address varchar (255),

City varchar (255)

)

You can name and define a CHECK constraint on multiple columns:

MySQL/ SQL Server/ Oracle/ Access

CREATE TABLE Clients

(

C_Id int NOT NULL,

Last varchar (255) NOT NULL,

First varchar (255),

Address varchar (255),

City varchar (255),

CONSTRAINT chk_Client

CHECK (C_Id 0 AND City= 'LosAngeles')

)

How to use the CHECK constraint on ALTER TABLE statement:

MySQL/ SQL Server/ Oracle/ Access

ALTER TABLE Clients

ADD CHECK (C_Id 0)

ALTER TABLE Clients

ADD CONSTRAINT chk_Clients

CHECK (C_Id 0 AND City= 'LasVegas')

How to DROP a CHECK constraint:

SQL Server/ Oracle/ Access

ALTER TABLE Clients

DROP CONSTRAINT chk_Clients

DEFAULT

How to use the DEFAULT constraint with CREATE TABLE statement:

CREATE TABLE Clients

(

Id int NOT NULL,

Last varchar (255) NOT NULL,

First varchar (255),

Address varchar (255),

City varchar (255)

DEFAULT 'LasVegas'

)

This will put a constraint on the "City" column when the "Clients" table is created. The DEFAULT constraint can even be used in order to insert system values by using functions such as GETDATE():

CREATE TABLE Orders

(

ID int NOT NULL,

OrderNo int NOT NULL,

C_Id int,

OrderDate date

DEFAULT GETDATE()

)

How to use the DEFAULT constraint with ALTER TABLE statement:

MySQL

ALTER TABLE Clients

ALTER City

SET DEFAULT 'LasVegas'

SQL Server/ Oracle/ Access

ALTER TABLE Clients

ALTER COLUMN City

SET DEFAULT 'LasVegas'

How to DROP a DEFAULT constraint:

MySQL

ALTER TABLE Clients

ALTER City DROP DEFAULT

SQL Server/ Oracle/ Access

ALTER TABLE Clients

ALTER COLUMN City DROP DEFAULT

NOT NULL

This will enforce a column to not accept a null value. By default, a column is able to hold null values. In order to enforce a field to always contain a value, the NOT NULL constraint can be used. Without having to add a value to this field, you won't be able to enter new data. How to use the NOT NULL constraint:

CREATE TABLE Clients

(

C_Id int NOT NULL,

Last varchar (255) NOT NULL,

First varchar (255),

Address varchar (255),

City varchar (255)

)

PRIMARY KEY

In order to be able to uniquely identify each record in a database table, the PRIMARY KEY constraint can be used. A null value can't be held in a primary key column. A primary key should be in each table. Each table can only have one primary key.

How to use PRIMARY KEY on CREATE TABLE statement:

MySQL
CREATE TABLE Clients

(

C_Id int NOT NULL,

Last varchar (255) NOT NULL,

First varchar (255),

Address varchar (255),

City varchar (255),

PRIMARY KEY (C_Id)

)

SQL Server/ Oracle/ Access
CREATE TABLE Clients

(

C_Id int NOT NULL PRIMARY KEY,

Last varchar (255) NOT NULL,

First varchar (255),

Address varchar (255),

City varchar (255)

)

In order to name and define a PRIMARY KEY constraint on multiple columns, use the following formula:

MySQL/ SQL Server/ Oracle/ Access

CREATE TABLE Clients

(

C_Id int NOT NULL,

Last varchar (255) NOT NULL,

First varchar (255),

Address varchar (255),

City varchar (255),

CONSTRAINT pk_PersonID PRIMARY KEY (C_Id,Last)

)

How to use the PRIMARY KEY on ALTER TABLE statement:

MySQL/ SQL Server/ Oracle/ Access

ALTER TABLE Clients

ADD PRIMARY KEY (C_Id)

Or the following can be used as well:

ALTER TABLE Clients

ADD CONSTRAINT pk_PersonID

PRIMARY KEY (C_Id,Last)

Keep in mind that when you use the ALTER TABLE statement that you also need to add a primary key. The columns must also already be declared to not be able to contain null values. This will be determined when the table is first created.

How to DROP a PRIMARY KEY constraint:

MySQL

ALTER TABLE Clients

DROP PRIMARY KEY

SQL Server/ Oracle/ Access

ALTER TABLE Clients

DROP CONSTRAINT pk_PersonID

FOREIGN KEY

The following statement will create a FOREIGN KEY on "C_Id" column when the "Orders" table is created. How to use FOREIGN KEY with CREATE TABLE statement:

MySQL

CREATE TABLE Orders

(

O_Id int NOT NULL,

OrderNo int NOT NULL,

C_Id int,

PRIMARY KEY (O_Id),

FOREIGN KEY (C_Id) REFERENCES Clients (C_Id)

)

SQL Server/ Oracle/ Access

CREATE TABLE Orders

(

O_Id int NOT NULL PRIMARY KEY

OrdersNo int NOT NULL,

C_Id int FOREIGN KEY REFERENCES Clients (C_Id)

)

In order to name a FOREIGN KEY constraint and to define a FOREIGN KEY for multiple columns, use the following formula:

```
CREATE TABLE Orders

(

O_Id int NOT NULL,

OrdersNo int NOT NULL,

C_Id int,

PRIMARY KEY (O_Id),

CONSTRAINT fk_PerOrders

FOREIGN KEY (C_Id)

REFERENCES Clients (C_Id)

)
```

How to use the FOREIGN KEY with the ALTER TABLE statement:

```
ALTER TABLE Orders

ADD FOREIGN KEY (C_Id)

REFERENCES Clients (C_Id)
```

This will create a FOREIGN KEY constraint on the "C_Id" column when the "Orders" table is already created.

ALTER TABLE Orders

ADD CONSTRAINT fk_PerOrders

FOREIGN KEY (C_Id)

REFERENCES Clients (C_Id)

This will name a FOREIGN KEY constraint and to define it also on multiple columns. How to DROP a FOREIGN KEY constraint:

MySQL

ALTER TABLE Orders

DROP FOREIGN KEY fk_PerOrders

SQL Server/ Oracle/ Access

ALTER TABLE Orders

DROP CONSTRAINT fk_PerOrders

UNIQUE

The UNIQUE constraint can be used to identify each record uniquely in a database. The UNIQUE and PRIMARY KEY constraints will both provide a certain amount of uniqueness for a set of columns or a column by itself. A PRIMARY KEY constraint will automatically have a UNIQUE constraint defined on it.

How to use the UNIQUE constraint on the CREATE TABLE statement:

MySQL

CREATE TABLE Clients

(

C_Id int NOT NULL,

Last varchar (255) NOT NULL,

First varchar (255),

Address varchar (255),

City varchar (255),

UNIQUE (C_Id)

)

SQL Server/ Oracle/ Access

CREATE TABLE Clients

(

C_Id int NOT NULL UNIQUE,

Last varchar (255) NOT NULL,

First varchar (255),

Address varchar (255),

City varchar (255)

)

In order to name a UNIQUE constraint and to define a UNIQUE constraint on multiple columns:

CREATE TABLE Clients

(

C_Id int NOT NULL,

Last varchar (255) NOT NULL,

First varchar (255),

Address varchar (255),

City varchar (255),

CONSTRAINT uc_PersonID

UNIQUE (C_Id,Last)

)

How to use the UNIQUE constraint on ALTER TABLE:

ALTER TABLE Clients

ADD UNIQUE (C_Id)

This is in order to create a UNIQUE constraint on the "C_Id" column when the table has already been created. In order to name a UNIQUE constraint and in order to define a UNIQUE constraint on multiple columns use the following formula below:

ALTER TABLE Clients

ADD CONSTRAINT uc_PersonID

UNIQUE (C_Id,Last)

In order to DROP a UNIQUE constraint:

MySQL

ALTER TABLE Clients

DROP INDEX uc_PersonID

SQL Server/ Oracle/ Access

ALTER TABLE Clients

DROP CONSTRAINT uc_PersonID

Using JOINS and FUNCTIONS in SQL

JOINS

In order to query data from two or more tables that are based on a relationship between certain columns in tables, the JOIN keyword can be used in an SQL statement. Keys allow tables in databases to be related to each other. Below is a list of the types of JOINS found in SQL:

- FULL JOIN- This will return the rows when there is a match in one of the tables.

- INNER JOIN- This will return rows when there is at least one match found in both tables.

- LEFT JOIN- This will return all the rows from the left table, even if there are no matches in the right table.

- RIGHT JOIN- This will return all the rows from the right side of the table, even if there are no matches in the left table.

FULL JOIN

SELECT column_name(s)

FROM table_name1

FULL JOIN table_name2

ON table_name1.column_name=table_name2.column_name

INNER JOIN

SELECT column_name(s)

FROM table_name1

INNER JOIN table_name2

ON table_name1.column_name=table_name2.column_name

It is important to note that an INNER JOIN is the same as the JOIN keyword.

LEFT JOIN

SELECT column_name(s)

FROM table_name1

LEFT JOIN table_name2

ON table_name1.column_name=table_name2.column_name

RIGHT JOIN

SELECT column_name(s)

FROM table_name1

RIGHT JOIN table_name2

ON table_name1.column_name=table_name2.column_name

FUNCTIONS

Some of these functions have been mentioned earlier in this book. Here, we will go over some of them and how to put them to use in a database. Listed below are some main functions:

Aggregate Functions

These types of functions will return a single value that is calculated from values in a column.

- AVG()- This will return the average value.

- COUNT()- This will return the number of rows.

- FIRST()- This will return the first value.

- LAST()- This will return the last value.

- MAX()- This will return the largest value.

- MIN()- This will return the smallest value.

- SUM()- This will return the sum.

Scalar Functions

- These types of functions will return a single value based on the input value.

- UCASE()- This will convert a field to upper case.

- LCASE()- This will convert a field to lower case.

- MID()- This will extract characters from a text field.

- LEN()- This will return the length of a text field.

- ROUND()- This will round a numeric field to the number of decimals specified.

- NOW()- This will return the current system date and time.

- FORMAT()- This will format how a field is to be displayed.

AVG()

SELECT AVG (column_name)

FROM table_name

An example of how you could use this more accurately in a table is if you have a list of prices for product held.

SELECT AVG (Price)

AS Average

FROM Orders

COUNT()

SELECT COUNT (column_name)

FROM table_name

COUNT(*)

This function will return the number of records in a table.

SELECT COUNT (*)

FROM table_name

COUNT (DISTINCT column_name)

SELECT COUNT (DISTINCT column_name)

FROM table_name

Keep in mind that this function will not work in Access.

FIRST()

SELECT FIRST (column_name)

FROM table_name

Here is an example of how the function works:

SELECT FIRST (Price)

AS FirstPrice

FROM Orders

FORMAT()

SELECT FORMAT (column_name, format)

FROM table_name

Here is an example of how to use this function when applying a date format:

SELECT Product, Price,

FORMAT(Now(), 'YYYY-MM-DD')

AS CurDate

FROM Products

This would add a column in a table that contains the current date.

LAST()

SELECT LAST (column_name)

FROM table_name

Here is an example of how this function would be used:

SELECT LAST (Price)

AS LastPrice

FROM Orders

LCASE()/ LOWER()

Here are the two ways that this function can be formatted:

SELECT LCASE(column_name)

FROM table_name

SELECT LOWER(column_name)

FROM table_name

Here is an example of how this function would be put to use:

SELECT LCASE(Last)

AS Last,First

FROM Clients

LEN()

SELECT LEN(column_name)

FROM table_name

Here is an example of how the function would be put to use:

SELECT LEN(City)

AS LengthOfCity

FROM Clients

MAX()

SELECT MAX(column_name)

FROM table_name

Here is an example of the function:

SELECT MAX(Price)

AS LargestPrice

FROM Orders

MID()

SELECT MID(column_name,start,[length])

FROM table_name

Here is an example of the function:

SELECT MID(City,1,3)

AS CityShort

FROM Clients

MIN()

SELECT MIN(column_name)

FROM table_name

Here is an example of how the function:

SELECT MIN(Price)

AS SmallestPrice

FROM Orders

NOW()

SELECT NOW ()

FROM table_name

Here is an example of the function:

SELECT Product, Price, Now()

AS CurDate

FROM Products

ROUND()

SELECT ROUND(column_name,decimals)

FROM table_name

Here is an example of the function:

SELECT Product, ROUND(Price,0)

as Price

FROM Products

SUM()

SELECT SUM(column_name)

FROM table_name

Here is an example of the function:

SELECT SUM(Price) AS Total

FROM Orders

UCASE()/ UPPER()

There are two ways that this function can be formed:

SELECT UCASE(column_name)

FROM table_name

SELECT UPPER(column_name)

FROM table_name

Here is an example of the function:

SELECT UCASE(Last)

as Last,First

FROM Clients

Conclusion

Although it can be much to learn, SQL can be a very simple language to use in a database. By taking advantage of the necessary tools in this book, you can successfully maneuver your way throughout any database. It is important to keep in mind that not all formulas work the same in every database and there are different versions listed in the book.

Although this has been written with examples of clients or inventory charts, there are many uses for databases. The examples given are not to be taken completely literal. You can use the information in this book to fit whatever your needs are for any database.

There is plenty to learn when it comes to SQL, but with the use of practice and good knowledge, you can be as successful as you decide to be in any database. Just how the English language has many rules to be followed, the same applies with SQL. By taking the time to thoroughly learn the language, many things are achievable with the use of a database. Refer back to any of the information in this book any time you are stumped on something you are working on.

Although it can be a complex challenge, patience and practice will help you successfully learn SQL. By remembering the basic commands and rules to SQL, you will avoid any issues that can come across most individuals that practice the use of it. It is a lot of information to take in, but instead, take it as it comes. Go to the practical tools that you may need for whatever you are trying to achieve through the database. When presented with an obstacle or complex assignment, refer to the tools that will clear up what you need. Take time to fully analyze what is before you while also trying to focus on one thing at a time.

Keep an open and simple mind when moving forward and you will keep any issues from becoming more complicated than what they need to be. As mention, SQL can be a simple thing to learn. You just need to take the time to understand what everything fully means in depth. If something doesn't turn out as expected, retrace your tracks to find where you might have inappropriately added a formula and some of the information. By building and maintaining successful problem-solving skills, you will not limit your success.

Thank you again for purchasing this book! I hope this book was able to help you thoroughly understand how SQL works. The next step is to put the tools and knowledge to use in your SQL database. Finally, if you enjoyed this book, please take the time to share your thoughts and post a review on Amazon. It'd be greatly appreciated!

Thank you and good luck!

About the Author

Nathan Clark is an expert programmer with nearly 20 years of experience in the software industry.

With a master's degree from MIT, he has worked for some of the leading software companies in the United States and built up extensive knowledge of software design and development.

Nathan and his wife, Sarah, started their own development firm in 2009 to be able to take on more challenging and creative projects. Today they assist high-caliber clients from all over the world.

Nathan enjoys sharing his programming knowledge through his book series, developing innovative software solutions for their clients and watching classic sci-fi movies in his free time.

To learn programming from an expert, look out for more of Nathan's books in store and online.

Made in the USA
Lexington, KY
02 August 2018